Marathon

Written by John Foster

Contents

Collins

What is a marathon?

These runners are taking part in a marathon.
A marathon is a race that's 42 **kilometres**
long (26 miles).

Marathons are held in many big cities.

Tokyo, Japan

New York, USA

Istanbul, Turkey

How marathons began

In 490BC the **Ancient Greeks** won a battle at a place called Marathon.

They sent a runner from Marathon to the city of Athens with the news that they had won.

He ran 42 kilometres. This is how the marathon got its name.

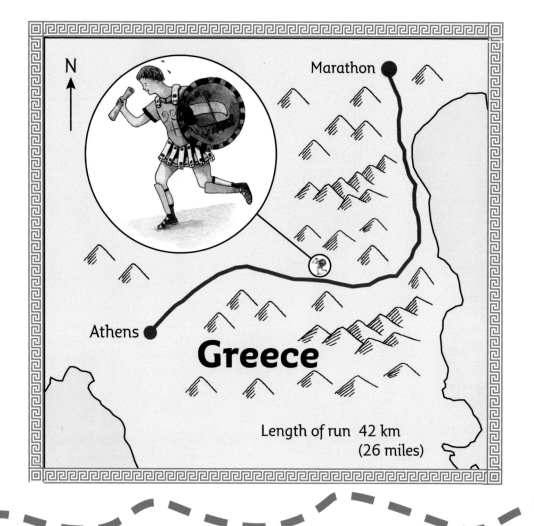

Length of run 42 km (26 miles)

The first marathon race was held at the **Olympic Games** in Athens in 1896. It was won by a Greek postman called Spiridon Louis.

In 1897, the American city of Boston held the first marathon that anybody could enter. The Boston marathon is still run today.

Nowadays, thousands of runners race in marathons. They can't all cross the start line at the same time.

The fastest runners start at the front and the other runners start further back.

Boston, USA

6

Rome, Italy

On the way

Marathon runners often pass famous buildings or cross famous bridges.
They can't stop to look!

the Empire State Building, New York

the Arc de Triomphe, Paris

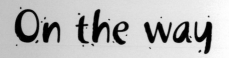

the London Eye, London

Keeping cool

People pass cups of water to the runners.

Running makes the runners **sweat** a lot. They pick up cups of water to drink and to pour over their heads, to cool down.

A marathon is a long race and some runners have to drop out. An ambulance is ready to help anyone who feels ill.

The winners

The winners cross the finishing line about two hours after they started.

Most people take three or four hours to finish the race.

Paula Radcliffe winning the London marathon

Hailu Negussie winning the Boston marathon

Yoko Shibui winning the Berlin marathon

13

Racing on wheels

People who use wheelchairs also race in marathons.

The fastest wheelchair racers can finish in less than two hours.

That's faster than the fastest runners!

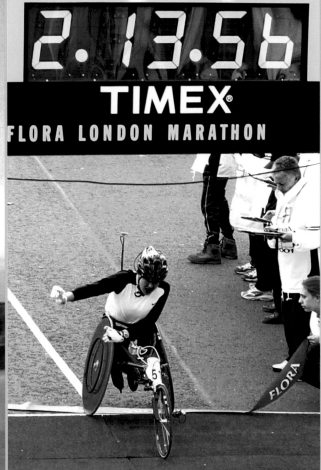

Dame Tanni Grey-Thompson winning
the London wheelchair marathon

Dressing up

A lot of people run marathons to raise money for **charity**.

Some of the runners dress up.

Rome

Boston

London

New York

Runners old and young

People from 18 to over 90 years old take part in marathons.

There are children's races for 11 to 17 year olds, called mini-marathons. The children run the last four kilometres (three miles) of the course.
Thousands of children take part in mini-marathons each year.

This man was 93 when he ran the London marathon.

Young and old runners take part in an Icelandic marathon.

The finish

Everyone who finishes a marathon gets a prize. The winners get medals, and other runners may get a certificate, a T-shirt or a goody bag.

Some people cross the finishing line hours after the winners.
But it doesn't matter how long it takes.
Finishing the race means that they have run 42 kilometres.
They have run a marathon.

This man took a whole week to finish a marathon!

Marathon facts

- The London and New York marathons are the largest in the world with about 40,000 runners each.
- Boston was the first marathon to include a wheelchair race in 1975.
- Running at a steady pace is more important than trying to overtake other runners.
- We sometimes use the word *marathon* to describe a long event.
- Some runners write their names on the front of their T-shirt so that the crowds can shout their name while they're racing!

Glossary

Ancient Greeks — people who lived in or near Greece from about 1,000BC to 146BC

charity — giving help, money or food to people in need

goody bag — a bag of small gifts

kilometre — 1,000 metres

Olympic Games — a sports competition held every four years in different parts of the world

sweat — When you sweat, drops of salty water come through your skin.

Index

🐾 Ideas for reading 🐾

Written by Clare Dowdall PhD
Lecturer and Primary Literacy Consultant

Learning objectives: pose questions and record these prior to reading; use a contents page to locate information; learn new words linked to a topic; use language and gesture when explaining ideas; present own work to members of the class

Curriculum links: Geography; Where in the World is Barnaby Bear; Citizenship: Taking part; PE: Athletic activities

Interest words: marathon, kilometres, Ancient Greeks, Olympic Games, famous, sweat, ambulance, wheelchairs, charity, certificate, goody bag

Word count: 504

Resources: small whiteboard and pen

Getting started

- Introduce the word *marathon* and ask the children if they know what it means. Share ideas, making reference to the front and back cover of the book.

- Explain that a marathon is a very long race that takes hours to complete, and that many people take part in it.

- Help children to raise questions about the marathon and record on a whiteboard. (*How far do runners run? How long does it take? How old do you have to be?*)

- Read the contents page together. Explain that contents are like headings and ask the children to suggest where they might find the answers to some of their questions.

Reading and responding

- Model how to use the contents to find an answer (e.g. using the introduction on p2 to find out basic information such as the distance of the race).

- Ask the children to read quietly and independently to p21, using a range of strategies to decode tricky words.

- Model how to use the glossary on p23 to discover the meaning of a word.